My First Space Books

EARTH and Our Solar System

by Francis Spencer

TABLE OF CONTENTS

A Crabtree Seedlings Book

Crabtree Publishing

crabtreebooks.com

Earth and Our Solar System

Earth is a **planet**.

It spins in space as part of our **solar system**.

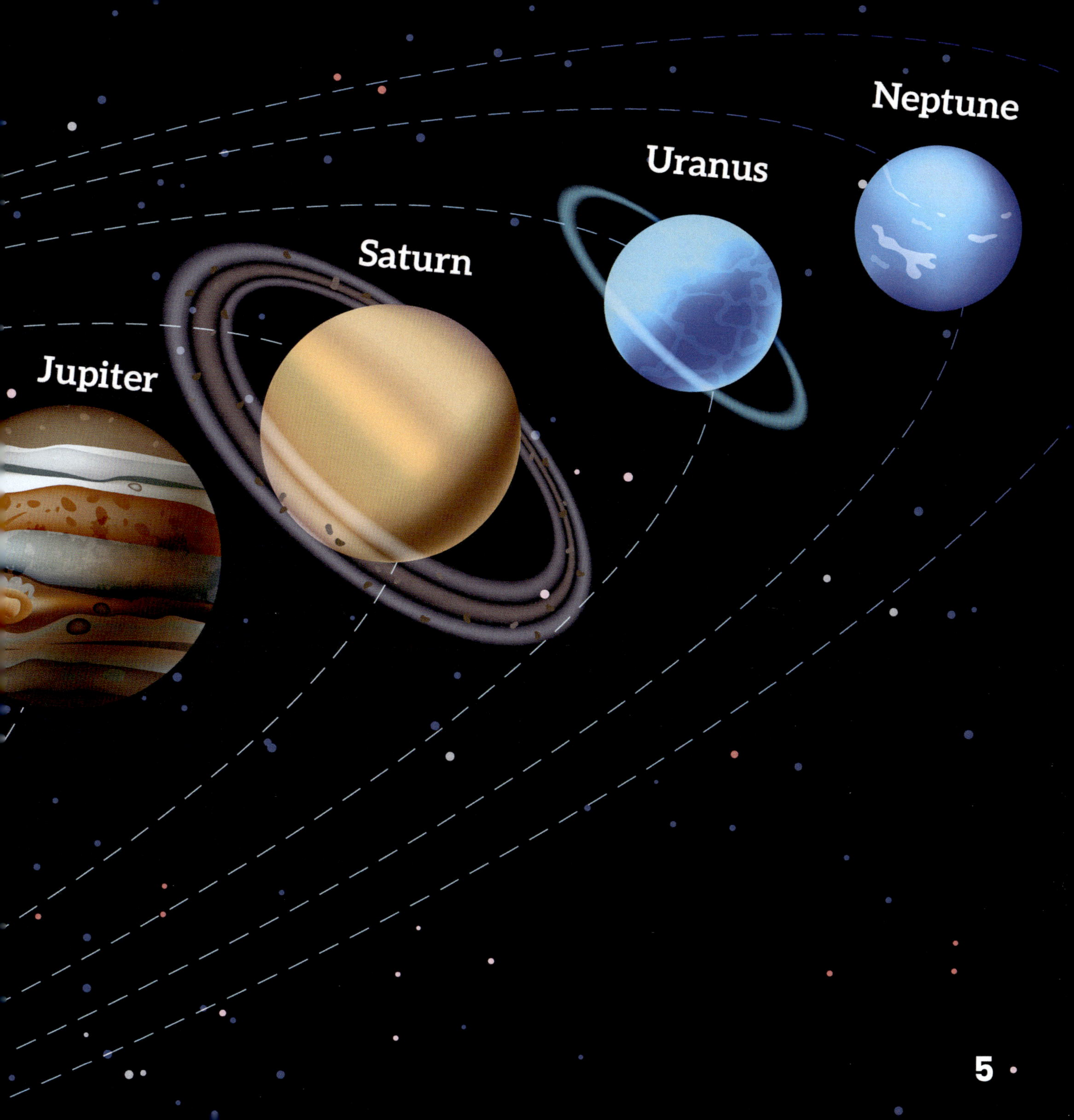
Neptune
Uranus
Saturn
Jupiter

It takes Earth a **whole day** to spin one time.

Because Earth spins, we get **daytime** and **nighttime**.

daytime

nighttime

It is daytime for the part of Earth facing the Sun.

It is nighttime for the part of Earth facing away from the Sun.

nighttime

Earth

Earth cannot leave our solar system.

It is held there by the Sun's **gravity**.

Earth

Our Moon is also part of our solar system.

Look at the picture.
Can you point to Earth?

Glossary

daytime (DAY-time): Daytime is the time between morning and evening when it is light outside.

gravity (GRAV-uh-tee): Gravity is the force that holds the planets in our solar system in their place around the Sun.

nighttime (NITE-time): Nighttime is the time between evening and morning when it is dark outside.

planet (PLAN-it): A planet is a large, round object that orbits, or travels around, the Sun. There are eight planets in our solar system.

solar system (SOH-lur SISS-tuhm): Our solar system is the Sun and the planets and space objects that move in orbit around it.

whole day (HOLE DAY): A whole day is measured from midnight to midnight and is 24 hours long.

Index

School-to-Home Support for Caregivers and Teachers

This book helps children grow by letting them practice reading. Here are a few guiding questions to help the reader build his or her comprehension skills. Possible answers appear here in red.

Before Reading

- **What do I think this book is about?** I think this book is about Earth and its position in the solar system. I think this book will explain the solar system.
- **What do I want to learn about this topic?** I want to learn more about outer space. I want to learn about what planet Earth is made of.

During Reading

- **I wonder why...** I wonder why Earth cannot leave our solar system. I wonder why it takes Earth one day to spin all the way around.
- **What have I learned so far?** I have learned that Earth is a planet. I have learned that because Earth spins, we get daytime and nighttime.

After Reading

- **What details did I learn about this topic?** I have learned that it is daytime for the part of Earth facing the Sun. I have learned that it is nighttime for the part of Earth facing away from the Sun.
- **Read the book again and look for the glossary words.** I see the word *planet* on page 3, and the word *gravity* on page 16. The other glossary words are found on pages 22 and 23.

Crabtree Publishing

crabtreebooks.com 800-387-7650

In Canada: We acknowledge the financial support of the Government of Canada through the Canada Book Fund for our publishing activities.

Hardcover 978-1-0396-6019-9
Paperback 978-1-0396-6214-8

Printed in Canada/022024/
CP20240215

Published in Canada
Crabtree Publishing
616 Welland Avenue
St. Catharines, Ontario
L2M 5V6

Published in the United States
Crabtree Publishing
347 Fifth Avenue
Suite 1402-145
New York, NY 10016

Written by: Francis Spencer
Print book version produced jointly with Blue Door Education in 2022
Photo Credits: Cover © Elena Schweitzer; pages 2-3 © buradaki; page 4-5 © Macrovector; page 6-7 © Triff; page 8-9 © Kellie L. Folkerts; page 10-11 and 12-13 © sebikus; page 14-15 © Naeblys; page 16-17 © Elena Schweitzer; page 18-9 © VINCENT GIORDANO PHOTO, page 20-21 © Triff. All images from Shutterstock.com

Library and Archives Canada Cataloguing in Publication
Available at the Library and Archives Canada

Library of Congress Cataloging-in-Publication Data
Available at the Library of Congress